PASTA & NOODLES

Quick and easy dishes from around the globe

CONTENTS

TECHNIQUES 4

RECIPES 6
Tomato sauce **6**
Spaghetti, Roman-style **8**
Pasta with flageolet beans, parsley, and lemon **10**
Spaghetti with pesto and pine nuts **12**
Pasta with aubergine sauce **14**
Spaghetti frutti di mare **16**
Spaghetti puttanesca **18**
Pasta with crab and lemon **20**
Pasta alla carbonara **22**
Pappardelle ragù **24**
Spinach and ricotta cannelloni **26**
Macaroni cheese **28**
Lasagne al forno **30**
Fideua **32**
Kässpätzle **34**
Hokkien noodles with char-sui pork **36**
Crispy rice noodles with beef **38**
Vietnamese beef and noodle salad **40**
Thai noodle stir-fry **42**
Pad Thai **44**
Singapore noodles **46**

ACKNOWLEDGEMENTS 48

Guide to symbols

The recipes in this book are accompanied by symbols that alert you to important information.

 Tells you how many people the recipe serves, or how much is produced.

 Indicates how much time you will need to prepare and cook a dish. Next to this symbol you will also find out if additional time is required for such things as marinating, standing, proving, or cooling. You need to read the recipe to find out exactly how much extra time is needed.

 Alerts you to what has to be done before you can begin to cook the recipe, or to parts of the recipe that take a long time to complete.

 Denotes that special equipment is required. Where possible, alternatives are given.

 Accompanies freezing information.

Techniques

Cook dried pasta

Dried pasta is a storecupboard essential, as it be used for many quick dishes.

1 Bring a large pan of salted water to the boil and gently pour in the pasta, allowing around 100g (3½oz) per person. Lower the heat, and simmer.

2 Cook for 10–12 minutes, or until firm to the bite (what the Italians call *al dente*). Drain through a colander, shaking to remove any excess water.

Boil noodles

Egg, wheat, or buckwheat noodles are quick to cook and great for stir-fries.

1 Bring a saucepan of water to the boil and add the noodles. Return to the boil, then cook until the noodles are softened and flexible – about 2 minutes.

2 Drain in a colander and rinse under cold, running water. Toss with a little oil to prevent them from sticking together, then continue with the recipe.

Peel and deseed tomatoes

Before using tomatoes for sauces or soups they must be peeled and deseeded.

1 Score an "X" in the skin at the base of each tomato, then immerse in a pan of boiling water for 20 seconds, or until the skin loosens.

2 Using a slotted spoon, remove the tomatoes from the boiling water and immediately plunge into a bowl of iced water to cool.

1 When cool enough to handle, use a paring knife to peel away the loosened skin, using the flat of the blade and your thumb.

2 Cut each tomato in half and gently squeeze each half over a bowl to extract the seeds. The flesh can now be chopped according to the recipe.

Tomato sauce

Easy to make, this sauce is wonderfully versatile.

INGREDIENTS

4 tbsp sunflower oil
1 onion, chopped
1 garlic clove, chopped
4 tbsp tomato purée
2 x 400g cans chopped tomatoes
8 basil leaves, torn
salt and freshly ground black pepper

METHOD

1 Heat the oil in a large saucepan over medium heat. Add the onion and garlic and fry, stirring occasionally, for 5–8 minutes, or until soft and golden.
2 Stir in the tomato purée, the tomatoes with their juice, half the basil leaves, and salt and pepper to taste. Lower the heat and simmer, uncovered, for 20 minutes, or until the sauce has thickened.
3 Stir in the remaining basil leaves just before serving.

makes 600ml (1 pint)

prep 5 mins • cook 30 mins

freeze for up to 1 month

Spaghetti, Roman-style

Quick to prepare and cook, this is a great meal when time is short.

INGREDIENTS

4 tbsp olive oil

2 small onions, thinly sliced

175g (6oz) pancetta or unsmoked back bacon, rind removed, and cut into thin strips

150ml (5fl oz) dry white wine

2 x 400g cans chopped tomatoes

salt and freshly ground black pepper

450g (1lb) dried spaghetti

150g (5½oz) mature pecorino cheese, grated

METHOD

1 Heat the oil in a large saucepan over a medium heat. Add the onions and fry, stirring, for 5 minutes, or until softened but not browned. Add the pancetta and continue frying, stirring, for 5 minutes, or until cooked through.

2 Add the wine and cook until reduces by half. Stir in the tomatoes and bring to the boil, then reduce the heat to low, and leave to bubble for 15 minutes or until blended and thickened. Season to taste with salt and pepper.

3 Meanwhile, bring a large pan of salted water to the boil over a high heat. Add the spaghetti, stir and boil for 10 minutes, or until the pasta is tender but firm to the bite. Drain the spaghetti well, then stir it into the sauce, making sure all the strands are coated. Sprinkle over the cheese, adjust the seasoning if necessary, and serve.

serves 4

prep 10 mins
• cook 15 mins

Pasta with flageolet beans, parsley, and lemon

This recipe uses a no-cook sauce – great when you want pasta fast.

INGREDIENTS

1 red onion, finely diced
400g can flageolet beans, drained
  and rinsed
handful of flat-leaf parsley,
  roughly chopped
1 garlic clove, grated or finely chopped
2 tbsp good-quality balsamic vinegar
zest of 1 lemon and juice of ½ lemon
salt and freshly ground black pepper
350g (12oz) dried orecchiette or other
  small pasta shells

METHOD

1 Place the first six ingredients in a large bowl and stir well to combine. Season well with salt and pepper. Leave to sit while you cook the pasta – the flavours will develop.
2 Cook the pasta in a large pan of boiling salted water for 10 minutes, or until it is cooked but still firm to the bite. Drain, keeping back a tiny amount of the cooking water. Return the pasta to the pan and toss together. Add the sauce, toss to combine, and serve.

serves 4

prep 10 mins
• cook 10 mins

Spaghetti with pesto and pine nuts

Store your fresh pesto in a jar topped with olive oil; it will keep in the refrigerator for up to a week.

INGREDIENTS
handful of basil
2 garlic cloves, chopped
50g (1¾oz) Parmesan cheese, grated
3 tbsp pine nuts, 1 tbsp toasted
4 tbsp olive oil
salt and freshly ground black pepper
350g (12oz) dried spaghetti

METHOD
1 Place the basil, garlic, Parmesan, and the 2 tablespoons of untoasted pine nuts in a food processor and whiz for a few seconds until combined. Scrape away from the sides, put the lid back on and, with the motor running, gently pour in the olive oil until you have a smooth paste. Season with salt and pepper.
2 Cook the pasta in a large pan of boiling salted water for 6 minutes or until it is cooked but still has a bit of bite to it. Drain, keeping back a tiny amount of the cooking water. Return the pasta to the pan and toss together. Gently toss with the pesto, then top with the toasted pine nuts and serve.

serves 4

prep 5 mins
• cook 12 mins

food processor

Pasta with aubergine sauce

Use large pasta shells so that the juicy sauce pools inside them.

INGREDIENTS

1 large aubergine, cut into cubes
salt and freshly ground black pepper
2–3 tbsp olive oil
½ small glass of red wine
1 onion, finely diced
2 garlic cloves, grated or
    finely chopped
400g can chopped tomatoes
pinch of dried oregano
1 tsp red pesto
350g (12oz) dried large pasta shells
Parmesan cheese, grated,
    to serve (optional)

METHOD

1 Place the aubergine cubes in a colander, and sprinkle well with salt. Cover with a plate, then place a heavy weight on top for 10 minutes to extract the bitter juices.

2 Heat the oil in a large frying pan, add the aubergine cubes, and cook over a medium heat for 4–6 minutes, or until they turn golden. Add the wine, raise the heat, and allow to boil for a couple of minutes. Stir in the onion and garlic and cook for a few seconds, then add the tomatoes and stir. Add the oregano and pesto, and simmer gently for 15 minutes.

3 Meanwhile, cook the pasta in a large pan of boiling salted water for 10 minutes, or until it is cooked but still has a bit of bite to it. Drain, keeping back a tiny amount of the cooking water. Return the pasta to the pan and toss together. Taste the sauce, and season with salt and black pepper. Toss with the pasta, sprinkle with grated Parmesan cheese (if using), and serve.

serves 4

prep 10 mins
• cook 25 mins

Spaghetti frutti di mare

A traditional spaghetti dish made with the season's freshest seafood.

INGREDIENTS

3 tbsp olive oil
1 small onion, finely chopped
2 garlic cloves, finely chopped
500ml (16fl oz) chunky passata
¼ tsp chilli flakes
450g (1lb) mussels, scrubbed
   and debearded
450g (1lb) baby squid, cleaned
   and tubes sliced into rings

4 tbsp dry white wine
½ lemon, sliced
450g (1lb) dried spaghetti
salt and freshly ground black pepper
12 large raw tiger prawns,
   peeled and deveined
3 tbsp chopped flat-leaf parsley

METHOD

1 Heat the oil in a large saucepan and fry the onion and garlic over a low heat, stirring, for 3–4 minutes, or until softened but not brown. Add the passata and chilli flakes, then simmer for 1 minute.

2 Meanwhile, place the mussels and squid in a large pan with the wine and lemon slices, cover tightly, and bring to the boil. Cook for 3–4 minutes, or until the shells have opened, shaking the pan occasionally. Remove from the heat, strain the liquid through a fine sieve and reserve. Discard the lemon slices and any unopened shells. Reserve a few mussels in their shells for garnishing and remove the rest from their shells.

3 Cook the spaghetti in a large pan of lightly salted boiling water for 10 minutes, or until cooked but still firm to the bite.

4 Meanwhile, add the reserved shellfish liquid to the sauce and simmer, uncovered, for 2–3 minutes, or until slightly reduced. Add the prawns to the sauce and simmer, stirring, for 2 minutes, or until just pink. Add the mussels and squid to the sauce, stir in the parsley, and season to taste with salt and pepper.

5 Drain the pasta thoroughly, return to the pan, and toss in the seafood and sauce. Tip into a large serving bowl, place the reserved mussels in their shells to the side of the pasta, and serve.

serves 4

prep 25 mins
• cook 20 mins

before cooking, tap the mussels and discard any that do not close

Spaghetti puttanesca

This spicy pasta dish is popular in Italy.

INGREDIENTS

4 tbsp extra virgin olive oil
2 garlic cloves, finely chopped
½ red chilli, deseeded and
  finely chopped
6 canned anchovies, drained and
  finely chopped
115g (4oz) black olives, pitted
  and chopped

1–2 tbsp capers, rinsed and drained
450g (1lb) tomatoes, skinned, deseeded,
  and chopped (see p5)
450g (1lb) dried spaghetti
handful of flat-leaf parsley, chopped, to serve
Parmesan cheese, grated, to serve

METHOD

1 Heat the oil in a saucepan, add the garlic and chilli, and cook gently for 2 minutes, or until the garlic is slightly coloured. Add the anchovies, olives, capers, and tomatoes and stir, breaking down the anchovies to a paste.
2 Reduce the heat and let the sauce simmer, uncovered, for 10–15 minutes, or until the sauce has thickened, stirring frequently.
3 Cook the spaghetti in plenty of lightly salted boiling water for 10 minutes, or until cooked but still firm to the bite. Drain.
4 Toss the spaghetti with the sauce, and serve sprinkled with parsley and Parmesan cheese.

serves 4

prep 15 mins
• cook 25 mins

Pasta with crab and lemon

Tangy lemon is a wonderful partner for the delicate flavours of the crab.

INGREDIENTS

1 tbsp olive oil
1 large onion, cut into quarters,
  then finely sliced
salt and freshly ground black pepper
2 garlic cloves, finely sliced
grated zest and juice of 1 lemon
handful of flat-leaf parsley,
  finely chopped
200g (7oz) fresh or canned white
  crabmeat
350g (12oz) dried linguine or spaghetti
chilli oil, to serve (optional)

METHOD

1 Heat the oil in a large frying pan, add the onion and a pinch of salt, and cook over a low heat for 5 minutes, or until soft and translucent. Stir in the garlic and lemon zest and cook for a few seconds more.
2 Stir through the parsley and crabmeat, then season well with salt and lots of black pepper. Add lemon juice to taste.
3 Meanwhile, cook the pasta in a large pan of boiling salted water for 6–8 minutes, or until it is cooked but still firm to the bite. Drain, keeping back a tiny amount of the cooking water. Return the pasta to the pan and toss together. Add the crab sauce, toss again, drizzle with chilli oil (if using), and serve.

serves 4

prep 5 mins
• cook 10 mins

Pasta alla carbonara

A creamy, flavourful Italian classic.

INGREDIENTS

450g (1lb) dried pasta, such as
  tagliatelle, spaghetti, or linguine
4 tbsp olive oil
175g (6oz) pancetta or cured unsmoked
  bacon rashers, rind removed, and
  finely chopped
2 garlic cloves, crushed
5 large eggs
75g (2½oz) Parmesan cheese,
  grated, plus extra to serve
75g (2½oz) pecorino cheese,
  grated, plus extra to serve
freshly ground black pepper
sprigs of thyme, to garnish

METHOD

1 Bring a large saucepan of salted water to the boil. Add the pasta, and bring to the
   boil for 10 minutes, or until the pasta is cooked but still firm to the bite.
2 Meanwhile, heat half the oil in a large frying pan over a medium heat. Add the
   pancetta or bacon and garlic and fry, stirring, for 5–8 minutes, or until the pancetta
   or bacon is crispy.
3 Beat the eggs and cheeses together and add black pepper to taste. Drain the pasta
   well and return to the pan. Add the eggs, pancetta, and the remaining oil, and stir
   until the pasta is coated. Serve while still hot, sprinkled with the extra cheese and
   garnished with sprigs of thyme.

serves 4–6

prep 10 mins
• cook 10 mins

Pappardelle ragù

Ragù is a rich, meaty, slow-simmered sauce.

INGREDIENTS

30g (1oz) butter
2 tbsp olive oil
100g (3½oz) pancetta, diced
1 small onion, finely chopped
1 celery stick, finely chopped
1 carrot, finely chopped
2 garlic cloves, crushed
400g (14oz) lean beef steak, minced

100ml (3½fl oz) beef stock
2 tbsp tomato purée
400g can chopped tomatoes
salt and freshly ground black pepper
75ml (2½fl oz) milk, warmed
450g (1lb) dried pappardelle pasta
Parmesan cheese, grated, to serve

METHOD

1 Melt the butter with the oil in a deep, heavy saucepan over a medium heat, and fry the pancetta for 1–2 minutes. Lower the heat, then add the onion, celery, carrot, and garlic, and continue to fry, stirring occasionally, for 10 minutes, or until softened but not browned.

2 Stir in the meat, breaking up any lumps, then cook for a further 10 minutes, or until it is evenly coloured, stirring frequently. Stir in the stock, tomato purée, and tomatoes, season to taste with salt and pepper, then bring to the boil.

3 Reduce the heat to very low, cover the pan, and simmer very gently for 1½hours. Stir occasionally to prevent sticking, adding more stock, if necessary. Stir the milk into the ragù, cover, and simmer for a further 30 minutes.

4 Bring a large pan of boiling, lightly salted water to the boil. Add the pappardelle and simmer for 8–10 minutes, or until cooked but still firm to the bite. Drain well, spoon the ragù over, and serve with freshly grated Parmesan.

serves 4

prep 15 mins
• cook 2 hrs 30 mins

freeze the sauce
for up to 3 months

Spinach and ricotta cannelloni

This vegetarian dish is an Italian classic.

INGREDIENTS

450g (1lb) cooked spinach
250g (9oz) ricotta cheese
1 egg, beaten
60g (2oz) Parmesan cheese, grated
pinch of freshly grated nutmeg
salt and freshly ground black pepper
16 cannelloni tubes

For the béchamel sauce

600ml (1 pint) full-fat milk
1 small onion
4 cloves
1 bay leaf

45g (1½oz) unsalted butter
45g (1½oz) flour
pinch of freshly grated nutmeg
salt and ground white pepper

For the Napoli sauce

1 tbsp extra virgin olive oil
1 small red onion, finely chopped
1 celery stick, finely chopped
2 garlic cloves, crushed
400g can chopped tomatoes
75ml (2½fl oz) vegetable stock
handful of basil leaves, torn

METHOD

1 Drain the spinach, pressing out any extra water, then chop roughly. Mix the ricotta, egg and half the Parmesan in a bowl. Mix in the spinach, then season with nutmeg, salt, and pepper. Spoon into the cannelloni tubes and place them in a lightly oiled baking dish.

2 To make the béchamel sauce, heat the milk in a pan with the onion, cloves, and bay leaf. Bring almost to the boil, then reduce the heat and simmer for 4–5 minutes. Set aside to cool completely. In another pan, melt the butter over a low heat. Stir in the flour and cook for 30 seconds. Remove pan from the heat and strain in the milk, whisking until the sauce is smooth. Return to the heat and cook, stirring constantly, until the sauce thickens. Stir in the nutmeg, and season with salt and white pepper.

3 To make the Napoli sauce, heat the oil in a saucepan, and gently cook the onion for 5–6 minutes, or until beginning to soften. Add the celery and garlic, cook for 2 minutes, then stir in the tomatoes and stock and simmer for 15 minutes, or until the vegetables are soft and the sauce has reduced a little. Stir in the basil.

4 Preheat the oven to 190°C (375°F/Gas 5). Pour the béchamel sauce over the cannelloni tubes, then spoon the Napoli sauce on top. Sprinkle over the remaining Parmesan. Bake for 35 minutes, or until golden and bubbling, and the cannelloni is cooked.

serves 4

prep 35 mins
• cook 35 mins

Macaroni cheese

This simple dish is a favourite family meal.

INGREDIENTS

400g (14oz) dried macaroni
85g (3oz) butter
100g (3½oz) fresh breadcrumbs
4 tbsp plain flour
1 tsp mustard powder
pinch of ground nutmeg
400ml (14fl oz) milk, warmed

175g (6oz) Cheddar cheese,
  coarsely grated
100g (3½oz) mozzarella cheese,
  drained and finely diced
60g (2oz) Parmesan cheese,
  coarsely grated

METHOD

1 Bring a large pan of lightly salted water to the boil over a high heat. Add the macaroni and boil for 2 minutes less than specified on the packet. Drain well and set aside, shaking off any excess water.

2 Meanwhile, preheat the oven to 200°C (400°F/Gas 6) and grease an ovenproof serving dish. Melt 25g (scant 1oz) of the butter in a small pan. Add the breadcrumbs, stir, then remove the pan from the heat and set aside.

3 Melt the remaining butter in a large saucepan over a medium heat. Sprinkle the flour over, then stir for 30 seconds. Stir in the mustard powder and nutmeg, then remove the pan from the heat and slowly whisk in the milk. Return the pan to the heat and bring the mixture to the boil, whisking, for 2–3 minutes, or until the sauce thickens. Remove from the heat. Stir in the Cheddar cheese, until melted and smooth, then add the macaroni and mozzarella and stir together.

4 Transfer the mixture to the prepared dish and smooth the surface. Toss the breadcrumbs with the Parmesan cheese and sprinkle over the top. Place the dish on a baking tray and bake for 25 minutes, or until heated through and golden brown on top. Leave to stand for 2 minutes, then serve.

serves 6

prep 20 mins
• cook 35 mins

Lasagne al forno

The perfect dish for family meals or casual entertaining.

INGREDIENTS

1 tbsp olive oil

1 large onion, chopped

2 celery sticks, chopped

2 small carrots, chopped

60g (2oz) pancetta, diced

500g (1lb 2oz) minced beef

400g can chopped tomatoes

1 tsp dried oregano

salt and freshly ground black pepper

50g (1¾oz) butter

50g (1¾oz) plain flour

600ml (1 pint) milk

150g (5½oz) ricotta cheese

12 pre-cooked lasagne sheets

50g (1¾oz) Parmesan cheese, grated

METHOD

1 To make the ragù sauce, heat the oil in a saucepan and sauté the onion, celery, carrots, and pancetta for 5 minutes, or until beginning to brown. Add the beef and cook until browned, breaking up with the side of a spoon. Add the tomatoes, oregano, and 150ml (5fl oz) water. Bring to the boil, then reduce the heat and simmer for 40 minutes. Season to taste.

2 Meanwhile, to make the béchamel sauce, melt the butter in a small saucepan and stir in the flour. Cook over a low heat, stirring, for 1 minute. Remove the pan from the heat and gradually beat in the milk. Return to the heat and cook, stirring constantly, until the sauce thickens. Season to taste with salt and pepper. Stir in the ricotta.

3 Preheat the oven to 190°C (375°F/Gas 5). Spread a little béchamel sauce over the base of the ovenproof dish. Arrange a layer of lasagne sheets on top, then add a third of the ragù sauce in an even layer. Drizzle 1 or 2 tablespoonfuls of the béchamel over the meat sauce and top with another layer of lasagne.

4 Repeat until all the lasagne and sauce has been used, finishing with a thick layer of béchamel sauce. Sprinkle Parmesan on top and bake for 45 minutes, or until piping hot and the sauce bubbles around the edge.

serves 4

prep 25 mins
• cook 1 hr 35 mins

20 × 30cm
(8 × 12in) shallow
ovenproof dish

Fideua

This Spanish pasta dish, with a tasty mixture of seafood, is hearty and filling.

INGREDIENTS

pinch of saffron threads
750ml (1¼ pints) hot fish stock
2–3 tbsp olive oil
1 onion, finely chopped
2 garlic cloves, crushed
3 ripe tomatoes, skinned, deseeded, and chopped (see p7)
1 tsp sweet paprika or smoked paprika
300g (10oz) dried spaghetti or linguine, broken into 5cm (2in) lengths
225g (8oz) raw prawns, peeled and deveined

8 small scallops, cut in half
12 clams, cleaned or mussels, scrubbed and debearded
225g (8oz) firm white fish, such as cod, haddock, or monkfish, cut into 2cm (¾in) pieces
140g (5oz) frozen peas
salt and freshly ground black pepper
2 tbsp chopped flat-leaf parsley

METHOD

1 Put the saffron threads in a small bowl and add 2 tablespoons of the hot fish stock. Set aside.

2 Heat the oil in a large frying pan or paella pan over a medium heat. Add the onion and garlic and fry for 5–8 minutes, or until soft and translucent, stirring frequently. Add the tomatoes and paprika and cook for a further 5 minutes. Add the saffron with its soaking liquid and half the remaining stock, increase the heat, and bring to the boil.

3 Add the spaghetti, reduce the heat, and simmer, uncovered, stirring occasionally for 5 minutes. Add the prawns, scallops, clams or mussels, white fish, and peas, and cook for a further 5 minutes, or until the pasta and fish are cooked through. If the mixture begins to dry out too much, add a little more stock. Discard any clams or mussels that have not opened. Season to taste with salt and pepper, sprinkle with the parsley, and serve hot.

serves 4

prep 15 mins
• cook 25 mins

before cooking, tap the clamsor mussels and discard any that do not close

Kässpätzle

Spätzle are a type of noodle popular in Switzerland; here it is tossed with eggs and cheese.

INGREDIENTS
400g (14oz) plain flour
1½ tbsp semolina or ground rice
6 eggs
100ml (3½fl oz) milk
½ tsp freshly grated nutmeg
60g (2oz) butter
115g (4oz) Gruyère cheese, grated
freshly ground black pepper
2 spring onions, finely sliced

METHOD
1 Sift the flour into a bowl and stir in the semolina. Lightly beat 4 eggs with the milk, nutmeg, and 100ml (3½fl oz) cold water. Add the egg mixture to the flour, mixing to make a slightly sticky elastic dough, adding more flour, if necessary.
2 Bring a large saucepan of water to the boil. Press the mixture through the holes of a colander (the holes should be medium-sized) over the saucepan, letting the noodles drop into the water. Take care to protect your hands from the steam.
3 Cook for 2–3 minutes, or until the noodles float to the top. Drain and run cold water over to stop them cooking any further. Drain again.
4 Heat the butter in a large frying pan, add the noodles, and toss over a low heat until coated and starting to turn golden. Sprinkle in the cheese; beat the remaining 2eggs and pour over the *spätzle*. Season to taste with black pepper and cook for 1–2 minutes, or until the cheese melts and the eggs set. Serve with the spring onions scattered over.

serves 4

prep 20 mins • cook 10 mins

colander with medium-sized holes

Hokkien noodles with char-sui pork

Char-sui is pork fillet marinated in hoisin, oyster sauce, and red pepper, then barbecued to give it a shiny scarlet glaze.

INGREDIENTS

45g (1½oz) dried Chinese mushrooms, such as Cloud Ear

2 tbsp oyster sauce

2 tbsp light soy sauce

1 tsp clear honey

2 tbsp groundnut oil or vegetable oil

2 garlic cloves, crushed

2 tsp finely grated fresh root ginger

1 red pepper, deseeded and finely sliced

140g (5oz) mangetout, halved lengthways

500g (1lb 2oz) fresh Hokkien noodles (thick egg noodles)

350g (12oz) char-sui pork, thinly sliced

METHOD

1 Put the mushrooms in a heatproof bowl, cover with boiling water, and set aside for 30 minutes to soak. Strain and cut the mushrooms into thin strips.

2 Simmer a large pan of water ready to cook the noodles. In a cup or small bowl, mix together the oyster sauce, soy sauce, and honey.

3 Heat the oil in a wok or large frying pan. Stir-fry the garlic and ginger for 30 seconds. Add the red pepper, stir-fry for 3 minutes, then add the mangetout and mushrooms, and stir-fry for 1 minute.

4 Drop the noodles into the pan of simmering water and cook for 1 minute, or until tender. Meanwhile, add the pork to the wok, pour in the oyster sauce mixture and toss over the heat for 1 minute, until everything is combined and piping hot. Drain the noodles, mix with the stir-fried pork and vegetables, and serve at once.

serves 4

prep 20 mins, plus soaking
• cook 10 mins

Crispy rice noodles with beef

A combination of crunchy textures and Asian flavours.

INGREDIENTS

groundnut oil, for frying
140g (5oz) dried rice vermicelli
2 tbsp oyster sauce
3 tbsp dark soy sauce
1 tbsp soft brown sugar
350g (12oz) sirloin steak, sliced
2 garlic cloves, thinly sliced

1 tsp grated ginger
12 thin asparagus spears, cut into
  2.5cm (1in) lengths
6 spring onions, cut into 2.5cm
  (1in) lengths
toasted sesame oil
2 tbsp roasted cashews, chopped

METHOD

1 Heat 5cm (2in) groundnut oil in a deep-fat fryer or large saucepan to 190°C (375°F) or until a piece of stale bread browns in less than 1 minute. Snip the vermicelli into short lengths and deep-fry in batches for a few seconds, or until white and crisp. Remove and drain well on kitchen paper. Keep warm.

2 Mix the oyster sauce, soy sauce, sugar, and 1 tablespoon of water. Set aside. Heat 2 tablespoons of groundnut oil in a wok over a high heat and stir-fry the beef for 2 minutes, or until browned. Remove and set aside.

3 Add a little more groundnut oil, and stir-fry the garlic and ginger for 30 seconds. Add the asparagus and spring onions, stir-fry for 2 minutes, then add the sauce, and return the beef to the wok. Cook for 1 minute, then drizzle with sesame oil.

4 Pile the stir-fry on top of the vermicelli, scatter with the cashews, and serve immediately.

serves 4

**prep 20 mins
• cook 15 mins**

**deep-fat fryer or
large saucepan • wok**

Vietnamese beef and noodle salad

Green papayas are under-ripe fruit that make a refreshing addition to many south-east Asian salads.

INGREDIENTS
350g (12oz) fillet steak, or thick
  rump steak
200g (7oz) rice vermicelli or mung
  bean noodles
250g (9oz) green papaya, peeled,
  deseeded, and cut into matchsticks
  or coarsely grated
4 tbsp roasted unsalted peanuts,
  coarsely chopped

For the dressing
1 tsp lemongrass purée
1 tsp finely grated fresh root ginger
2 tbsp chopped coriander
2 tbsp Vietnamese nuoc mam or
  Thai fish sauce
2 tbsp chopped mint
juice of 2 limes
1 tsp brown sugar
2 red chillies, deseeded and
  finely chopped

METHOD
1 Preheat the grill to high. Trim any fat from the steak and grill for 3–4 minutes on each side, or until browned but still pink in the centre. Set aside for at least 15 minutes before slicing into thin strips.
2 Soak the vermicelli in boiling water until softened, or as directed on the packet. Drain, rinse in cold water, then cut into manageable lengths with kitchen scissors. Set aside.
3 To make the dressing, mix together the lemongrass purée, ginger, coriander, fish sauce, mint, lime juice, sugar, and chillies.
4 Pile the noodles, papaya, and steak into a serving dish and add the dressing. Toss lightly together and scatter with peanuts before serving.

serves 4

prep 20 mins,
plus standing
• cook 8 mins

Thai noodle stir-fry

A fragrant and colourful stir-fry with the flavours of Thailand.

INGREDIENTS

175g (6oz) thin rice noodles
1 stalk lemongrass
3 tbsp groundnut oil or vegetable oil
3 skinless boneless chicken breasts,
  cut into thin strips
1 onion, sliced
1 tsp finely grated fresh root ginger

1 red chilli, deseeded and finely chopped
1 orange pepper, deseeded and sliced
115g (4oz) shiitake mushrooms, sliced
2 heads of pak choi, shredded
2 tbsp light soy sauce
1 tbsp Thai fish sauce, such as nam pla
1 tsp sweet chilli sauce

METHOD

1 Soak the noodles in a bowl of boiling water until softened, or as directed on the packet.
   Drain and set aside. Meanwhile, remove and discard the outer leaves of the lemongrass
   and trim away the tough woody end. Finely chop.

2 Heat 2 tablespoons of the oil in a wok and stir-fry the chicken over a high heat for
   2–3 minutes, or until lightly browned. Remove from the pan and set aside.

3 Reduce the heat to medium, add the remaining oil, and stir-fry the onion for
   2 minutes. Add the lemongrass, ginger, chilli, orange pepper, and mushrooms,
   and stir-fry for 2 minutes.

4 Add the pak choi and stir-fry for a further 2 minutes, then return the chicken to the
   pan and add the noodles. Pour in the soy sauce, fish sauce, and sweet chilli sauce,
   and toss everything together over the heat for 2–3 minutes, or until piping hot and
   the chicken is cooked through. Serve at once.

serves 4

**prep 20 mins
• cook 15 mins**

wok

Pad Thai

This is one of Thailand's national dishes, where it is often served rolled up in a thin omelette.

INGREDIENTS

2 tbsp chopped coriander

1 red Thai chilli, deseeded and finely chopped

4 tbsp vegetable oil

250g (9oz) raw tiger prawns, peeled and deveined

4 shallots, finely chopped

1 tbsp sugar

4 large eggs, beaten

2 tbsp oyster sauce

1 tbsp Thai fish sauce, such as nam pla

juice of 1 lime

350g (12oz) flat rice noodles, cooked according to packet instructions

250g (9oz) beansprouts

4 spring onions, sliced

115g (4oz) unsalted roasted peanuts, coarsely chopped

1 lime, cut into 4 wedges, to serve

METHOD

1 Mix together the coriander, chilli, and vegetable oil. Heat half the mixture in a wok, add the prawns, and stir-fry for 1 minute. Remove and set aside.

2 Add the remaining herb oil to the wok and stir-fry the shallots for 1 minute. Add the sugar and the eggs, and cook for 1 minute, stirring frequently to scramble the eggs as they begin to set.

3 Stir in the oyster sauce, fish sauce, lime juice, cooked noodles, and beansprouts, and return the prawns to the wok. Stir-fry for 2 minutes, then add the spring onions and half the peanuts. Toss everything together for 1–2 minutes, or until piping hot.

4 To serve, divide between 4 individual bowls, scatter the remaining peanuts on top, and add a lime wedge.

serves 4

prep 20 mins • cook 10 mins

wok

Singapore noodles

This popular dish combines the delicacy of Chinese cooking, the heat of Indian spices, and the fragrance of Malay herbs.

INGREDIENTS

2 tbsp vegetable oil

140g (5oz) skinless boneless chicken breasts, cut into thin strips

140g (5oz) raw prawns, peeled and deveined

1 onion, thinly sliced

½ red pepper, deseeded and cut into strips

1 head of pak choi, thinly sliced

2 garlic cloves, finely chopped

1 red chilli, deseeded and finely chopped

115g (4oz) beansprouts

1 tbsp curry paste

2 tbsp light soy sauce

150g (5½oz) vermicelli egg noodles, cooked according to the packet instructions

2 large eggs, beaten

coriander, to garnish

METHOD

1 Heat half the oil in a wok, add the chicken, and stir-fry for 1 minute. Add the prawns and stir-fry for another 2 minutes. Remove the chicken and the prawns from the wok and set aside.

2 Add the rest of the oil to the wok and stir-fry the onion for 2 minutes, then add the red pepper, pak choi, garlic, and chilli and cook for a further 2 minutes.

3 Tip in the beansprouts, stir-fry for 30 seconds, then stir in the curry paste and soy sauce and stir-fry for 1 minute. Add the noodles, pour in the eggs, and toss everything together over the heat for 1 minute, or until the egg starts to set.

4 Return the chicken and prawns to the wok and stir-fry for 1 minute. Serve with the coriander scattered over.

serves 4

prep 15 mins • cook 10 mins

wok

London, New York, Melbourne, Munich, and Delhi

Editor Cécile Landau

Jacket Designer Mark Penfound

DTP Designer Kavita Varma

DK INDIA

Editorial Consultant Dipali Singh

Designer Neha Ahuja

DTP Designer Tarun Sharma

DTP Coordinator Sunil Sharma

Head of Publishing Aparna Sharma

First published in Great Britain in 2013.
Material in this publication was previously published
in *The Cooking Book* (2008) and *Cook Express* (2009)
by Dorling Kindersley Limited
80 Strand, London WC2R 0RL
Penguin Group (UK)

A CIP catalogue record for this book is available
from the British Library.

ISBN 978-1-4093-2597-0

Printed and bound in China by Hung Hing Printing Co. Ltd.